FABRIGAMI

THE ORIGAMI ART OF FOLDING CLOTH
TO CREATE DECORATIVE AND USEFUL OBJECTS

JILL STOVALL, SCOTT STERN and FLORENCE TEMKO

TUTTLE Publishing

Tokyo │ Rutland, Vermont │ Singapore

The Tuttle Story: "Books to Span the East and West"

Many people are surprised to learn that the world's largest publisher of books on Asia had its humble beginnings in the tiny American state of Vermont. The company's founder, Charles E. Tuttle, belonged to a New England family steeped in publishing.

Immediately after WW II, Tuttle served in Tokyo under General Douglas MacArthur and was tasked with reviving the Japanese publishing industry. He later founded the Charles E. Tuttle Publishing Company, which thrives today as one of the world's leading independent publishers.

Though a westerner, Tuttle was hugely instrumental in bringing a knowledge of Japan and Asia to a world hungry for information about the East. By the time of his death in 1993, Tuttle had published over 6,000 books on Asian culture, history and art—a legacy honored by the Japanese emperor with the "Order of the Sacred Treasure," the highest tribute Japan can bestow upon a non-Japanese.

With a backlist of 1,500 titles, Tuttle Publishing is more active today than at any time in its past—inspired by Charles Tuttle's core mission to publish fine books to span the East and West and provide a greater understanding of each.

Published by Tuttle Publishing, an imprint of Periplus Editions (HK) Ltd.

www.tuttlepublishing.com

Library of Congress Cataloging-in-Publication Data

Stovall, Jill.
Fabrigami : the origami art of folding cloth to create beautiful craft objects / Jill Stovall, Florence Temko, and Scott Wasserman Stern. -- First edition.
    pages cm
ISBN 978-4-8053-1256-8 (paperback)
1. Fabric folding (Textile crafts) 2. Origami. I. Temko, Florence. II. Stern, Scott Wasserman. III. Title.
TT840.F33S76 2013
736'.982--dc23
                2013016971

ISBN 978-4-8053-1256-8

Distributed by

North America, Latin America & Europe
Tuttle Publishing
364 Innovation Drive,
North Clarendon,
VT 05759-9436 U.S.A.
Tel: 1 (802) 773-8930
Fax: 1 (802) 773-6993
info@tuttlepublishing.com
www.tuttlepublishing.com

Asia Pacific
Berkeley Books Pte. Ltd.
61 Tai Seng Avenue #02-12,
Singapore 534167
Tel: (65) 6280-1330
Fax: (65) 6280-6290
inquiries@periplus.com.sg
www.periplus.com

First edition
16 15 14 13   5 4 3 2 1
1307EP
Printed in Hong Kong

CONTENTS

ACKNOWLEDGMENTS

Florence Temko and I began work on this book before she passed away. She left an international community of admirers. She was a delightful friend and a brilliant artist. All who knew her will miss her. She popularized the word "Kirigami," that is now a common term for cutting folded paper. Ever forward thinking, Florence became interested in finding the best way to create folded fabric. We both tried various techniques and found the perfect stiffening formula to apply to fabric so that it could be folded like paper—the result is the BEAUTIFUL ART of FABRIGAMI.

We now introduce FABRIGAMI!

Pre-stiffened fabric can be used for all of the paper craft techniques that we love such as origami, kirigami, and scrapbooking.

I am enormously grateful for the tremendous support from Robert Lang a distinguished origami artist who took the time to encourage the completion of this book and make suggestions for collaborations and proper origami techniques.

Scott Stern the illustrator is a most gifted young man who designed his first model at the age of six, and, at eighteen, published his own book of original origami creations. Not only did he illustrate all of the models here, but also folded them for the photographs and designed several of the models in the book himself.

A special thank you to David Cooper who was able to create beautiful photographs using Scott's models.

Finally, I am most grateful to my family and friends for their support and encouragement.

Folding doesn't have to be confined to paper and cloth, you can also fold won ton wrappers or even tortillas. David Lister, an origami artist, author, and creator, compiled a list of materials that are origami compatible. These materials include rubber balloons, metal, rayon mesh, celluloid, fruit leather and other material that you would not associate with origami.

FABRIGAMI is just one more creative adventure into the world of folding crafts that has brought so much fun to all ages and cultures. The models are traditional or original creations.

Special thanks to my wonderful, creative, and reliable test team at Transition Services, Inc. Las Vegas, NV. TSI provides meaningful work for people with developmental disabilities.
Visit www.tsilasvegas.com

AN INTRODUCTION TO FABRIGAMI

Although "Origami" is a Japanese word—"ori" means to fold and "gami" means paper, here we have created a new word for folding fabric: Fabrigami.

The delightful designs and colors of fabric have always offered an irresistible lure for crafters. Elaborate quilts, scrapbook covers, and jewelry projects are just some of the ways crafters use fabric. But, when we add the dimension of paper crafting techniques, then fabric has a new life. As Scott Stern, the origami artist and author, remarked to me "…more and more I see how the beauty of the fabric is what really accentuates these folded creations." With so many variations of fabric available in the world, I think you will find these models to be a great way to make folded cloth projects that are both durable and beautiful.

Figure 1
Stiffening
Liquid

ONLINE RESOURCES

For Fabric Squares:

http://www.etsy.com/shop/materialgirlchic

http://www.keepsakequilting.com

http://www.hawaiianfabricshop.com/fabricsquares.html

http://www.fabric.com/

Premade Fabric Stiffeners:

http://www.diptichemicals.net/stiffy-coldfabric-stiffener.html

PREPARING THE CLOTH

Fabric Selection

Most light cotton or cotton blend fabrics work well for the stiffening and folding process. Very delicate and slick fabrics such as silk can stain and don't fold well. Very coarse or heavy fabric, like corduroy or velvet, should also be avoided. Many quilt stores sell a variety of pre-cut fabric squares that are popularly known as "fat quarters." These packages give you a nice selection of complementary colors and are very reasonable in price. Otherwise, you should cut fabric to your required square size before treatment.

Remember to use caution with scissors and cutting utensils.

Stiffening the Cloth to Hold

Your objective is to apply stiffening agent to the fabric that will allow it hold the fold. Your choice of product is largely determined by the project and what you expect from the fabric. A project with many complicated folds requires a light but stiff coating of a liquid adherent. You can choose from several commercial stiffening products like a spray starch or a specifically made brand product like Stiffy. Easier folds can be achieved by bonding fabric with fusible web products, such as Wonder Under. There are many new machines such as the xyron available for cutting and bonding as well.

Some scrapbook stores make laminating and sticker machines available for customer use during certain hours of the day.

These commercial products are available in most craft stores. Remember to read instructions and use adequate ventilation.

Iron Out the Details

Any wrinkles in your square piece of fabric should be pressed out using a press cloth and warm iron.

Getting wrinkles out is much easier before treatment.

SECRET FORMULA and Liquid Adherent Instructions

The secret formula came about as our test team sought the formula for the easiest, cheapest, and most reliable liquid adherent product. The fabrics used for the projects in this book were treated using the following formula:

Secret Formula
- 4 cups (1 liter) water
- 1 cup (250 ml) Elmer's Glue-All

You will be able to treat about a yard of material with this combined amount.

Materials List
- Cotton or cotton blend fabric
- Fabric stiffener or SECRET FORMULA
- Water
- Large bowl for mixing and dipping
- Whisk or fork to stir
- Iron
- Cutting Tools
- Hanging rack or a clean slick area for drying the cloth (Plastic garbage bag or tinfoil can be used)

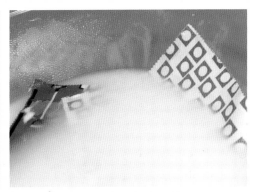

Step 1: Cut and iron your fabric

Step 2: Prepare the Formula

Step 3: Immerse the cloth in the Formula or stiffening agent.

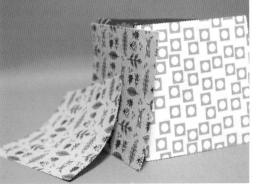

Step 4: Smooth excess liquid with your fingers as you remove it from the bowl.

Step 5: Hang them to dry on a line or rod

Your finished product will look like this.

Last Minute Gifts

MAXIMIZE—Many of these projects are suitable for a grand scale installations as wall art, centerpieces, or wall hangings. You can cluster creations of different colors to create stunning murals or displays.

MINIMIZE—Popular origami trends indicate challenges on a microscale, so for some of these projects you can go small and make smaller items that can be used as hairclips, earrings, pins, charms, hat decorations, and even attached to flip flops or crocs.

You can easily impress your friends and relatives with these charming, handmade, and artistic creations. Half the fun is choosing the fabric to personalize the gift to match favorite colors, hobbies, interests, or decor. This makes fabrigami a great way to make something thoughtful, unique, and beautiful.

FOLDING BASICS

VALLEY FOLD

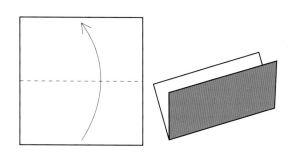

Fold the paper, forming a valley-like depression.

MOUNTAIN FOLD

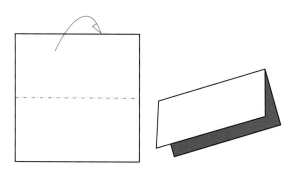

Fold the paper, forming a mountain-like protrusion.

FOLD AND UNFOLD

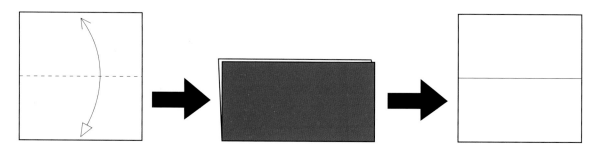

Fold the paper, forming a crease. Once the crease is complete, unfold the paper back to its original position.

SINK FOLD

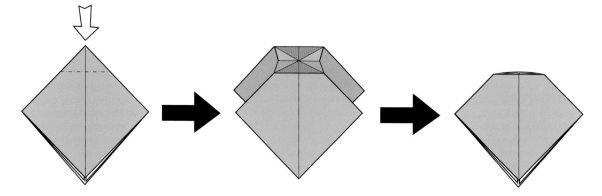

Open the paper and invert the tip, pressing it down into the model. As you are pressing the tip down, reverse the creases surrounding the tip, forming a square of mountain folds.

SQUASH FOLD

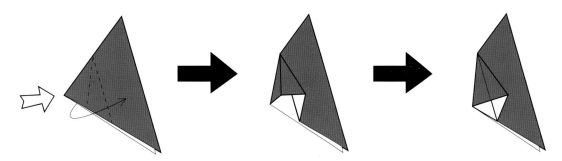

Open up one corner of the paper, swinging what was formerly a creased edge over and pressing it down.

....

PLEAT FOLD

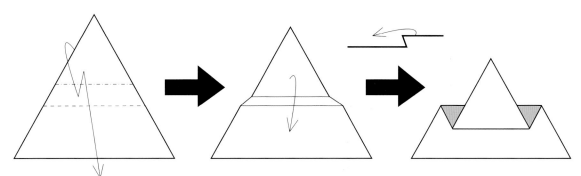

Valley fold the top of tip down to a given point.
Then fold the tip back up to a point slightly lower than the original position.

....

REVERSE FOLD

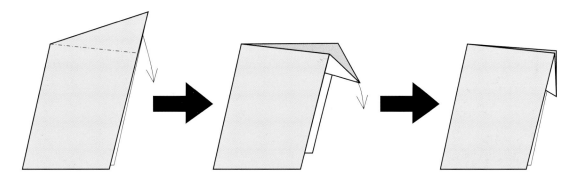

Spread the top of the model and reverse the creases, mountain folding the top corner down and in.
Collapse the model while pulling the reversed corner down.

....

RABBIT EAR FOLD

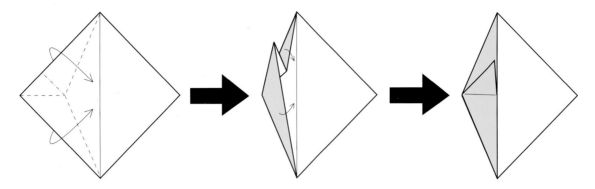

Collapse one side, so that the left edges will lie even with the center crease. To do this, make two valley creases; at the point at which they meet, make another valley crease up to a corner of the paper. The crease should thus collapse.

PETAL FOLD

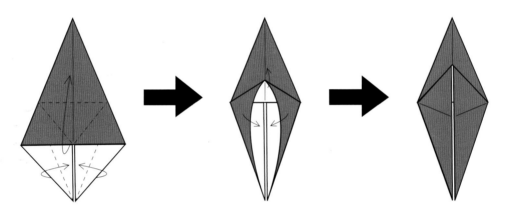

Bring the two sides into the center while swinging the bottom of the colored flap up, forming a point in the center of the flap. The left and right sides will now lie even with the center.

REVIEW OF IMPORTANT SYMBOLS

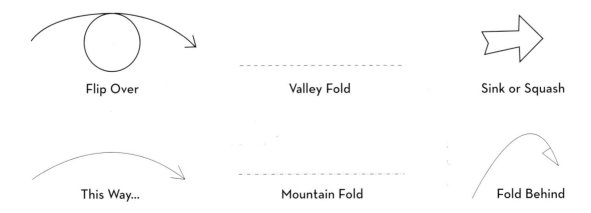

Flip Over

Valley Fold

Sink or Squash

This Way...

Mountain Fold

Fold Behind

OTHER BASIC FOLDS

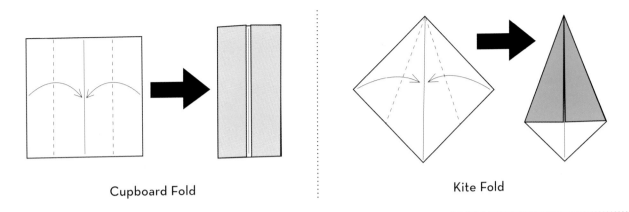

Cupboard Fold

Kite Fold

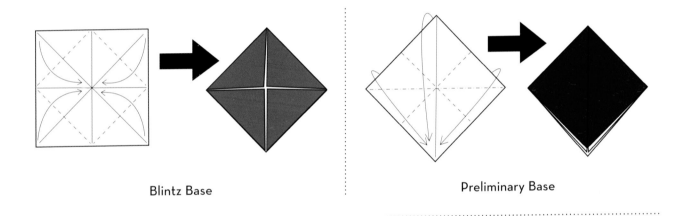

Blintz Base

Preliminary Base

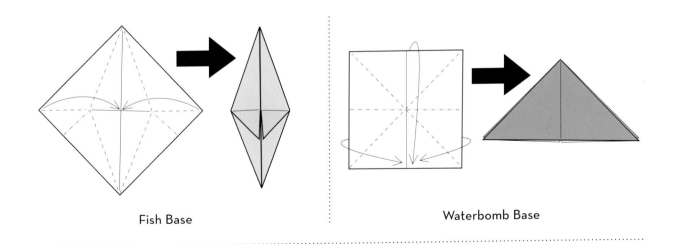

Fish Base

Waterbomb Base

BILLFOLD AND BUSINESS CARD HOLDER

This simple wallet with two compartments can be made in two different sizes to suit dollar bills or business cards. The folding procedure is identical for both.

You will need:

A 13 inches (33 cm) stiffened fabric square for a billfold, or An 8 inches (20 cm) stiffened fabric square for business cards

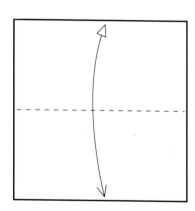

1 Begin with the inside of the fabric facing up. Valley fold in half vertically. Then unfold.

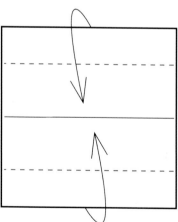

2 Valley fold the top and bottom edges almost to the crease. Leave a little gap in between the two edges.

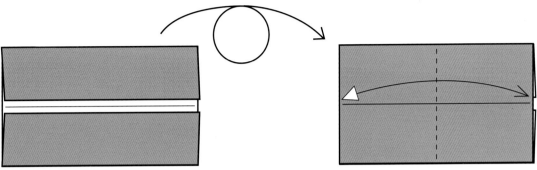

3 Flip the model over.

4 Valley fold the model in half. Then unfold.

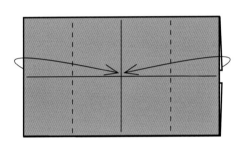

5 Valley fold the two edges to the center crease.

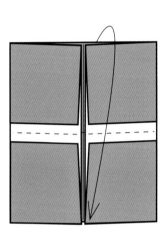

6 Valley fold the top edge down.

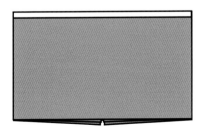

6 The completed billfold and business card case.

Tip: If the billfold does not open at the top, then check step 5 to make sure you folded in half in the right direction.

Other currencies: For other bill denominations, begin with a square with sides twice the width of the bill, plus ½ inch (1 cm) extra.

BIRD OF PEACE

The origami crane is a recognized symbol of peace, many people send paper cranes to family and friends to express their good wishes. This fabric version will make a durable and beautiful version of this origami staple.

You will need:
A square of stiffened fabric in whatever size you want for your project.

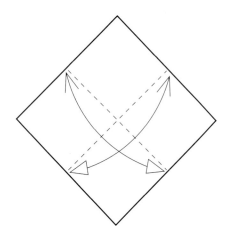

1 Begin with the inside of the fabric facing up. Valley fold in half vertically. Then unfold.

2 Valley fold the top and bottom edges almost to the crease. Leave a little gap in between the two edges.

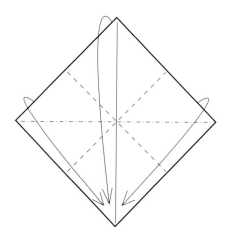

3 Begin with the inside of the fabric facing up. Valley fold in half vertically. Then unfold.

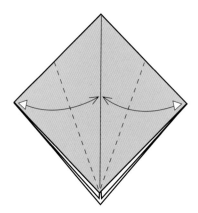

4 Valley fold the top and bottom edges almost to the crease. Leave a little gap in between the two edges.

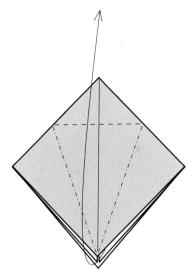 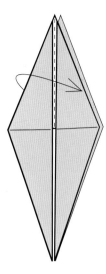 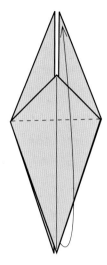

5 Begin with the inside of the fabric facing up. Valley fold in half vertically. Then unfold.

6 Valley fold the top and bottom edges almost to the crease. Leave a little gap in between the two edges.

7 Begin with the inside of the fabric facing up. Valley fold in half vertically. Then unfold.

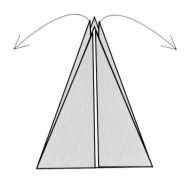 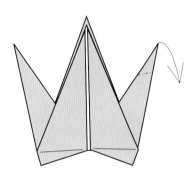 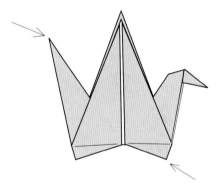

8 Valley fold the top and bottom edges almost to the crease. Leave a little gap in between the two edges.

9 Begin with the inside of the fabric facing up. Valley fold in half vertically. Then unfold.

10 Valley fold the top and bottom edges almost to the crease. Leave a little gap in between the two edges.

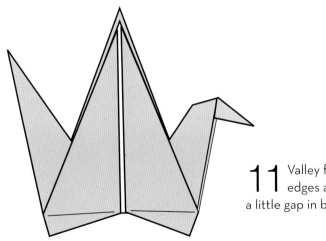

11 Valley fold the top and bottom edges almost to the crease. Leave a little gap in between the two edges.

DECORATIVE BLOOMS

This is a wonderful decorative item that can be used on gift boxes, as a decorative pin, or as part of a garden centerpiece for the dinner table.

You will need:
A square of stiffened fabric: a 6 inches (15 cm) square results in a 4 inches (10 cm) bloom.

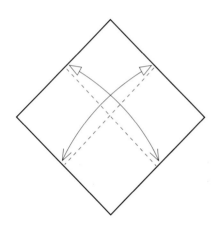

1 Begin with the paper side facing up. Valley fold in half from corner to corner. Repeat on the other side. Then unfold.

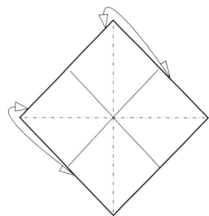

2 Mountain fold the square in half to the back in both directions. Then unfold.

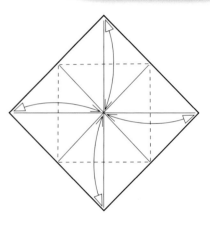

3 Valley fold all four corners to the center. Then unfold.

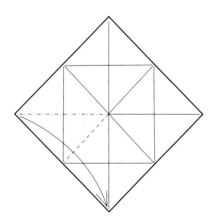

4 Guide the left corner down to the bottom, collapsing the model, which will not lie flat.

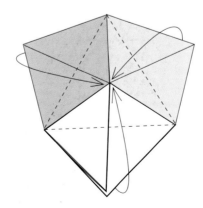

5 Valley fold the three corners into the center.

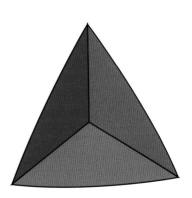

6 The completed bloom.

BUTTERFLIES

These butterflies can be spread randomly on a party table or placed on top of glasses. Either way, they make fine party favors that guests will be delighted to take home.

You will need:

*A stiffened fabric square
6 inches (15 cm) sides
A stiffened fabric square
4½ inches (11 cm) sides
A wire twist or chenille stem
(pipe cleaner)*

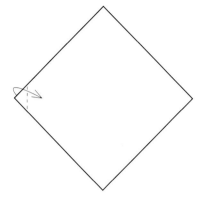 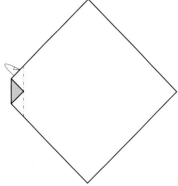 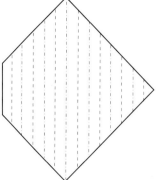

1 Valley fold one corner over a little bit along the diagonal.

2 Mountain fold the corner behind at its edge.

3 Continue folding the corner back and forth, pleating the entire model diagonally.

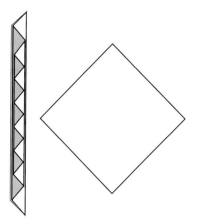  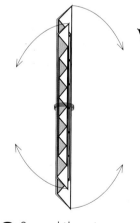 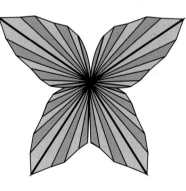

4 Repeat steps 1 – 3 on the other sheet.

5 Tie the pleated squares together at the center with the wire twist. Allow the ends of each to hang freely.

6 Spread the wings by pulling the four corners apart and letting the layers spread. Let the larger wings rest on the top, with the smaller wings on the bottom.

7 The completed butterfly.

Mobile: Suspend butterflies of different sizes from different heights.

BOOKMARKS

These bookmarks are very popular items for gifts and for selling at fundraisers and bazaars.

You will need:
*A strip of stiffened fabric 30 x 1½ inches
   (75 x 4 cm)*
Scissors

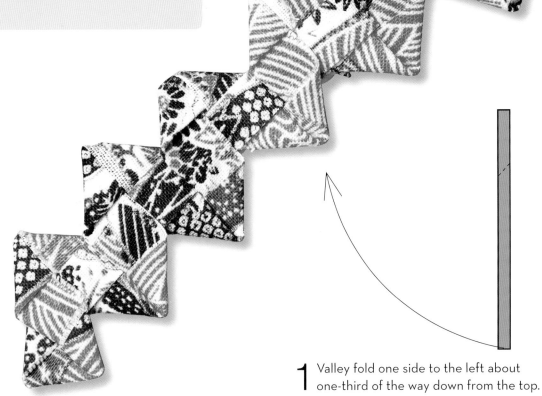

1 Valley fold one side to the left about one-third of the way down from the top.

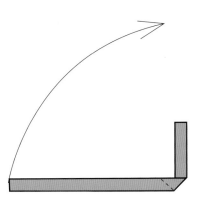

2 Valley fold the flap up so that it lies even with the smaller flap.

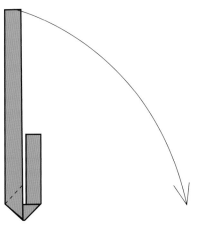

3 Valley fold the flap up so that it lies even with the smaller flap.

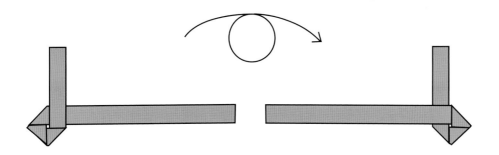

4 Flip the model over.

5 Repeat steps 2–4 on left flap.

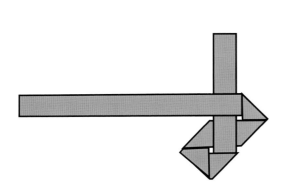

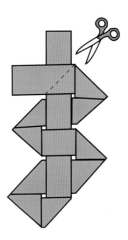

6 Repeat steps 2–5 on left flap.

7 Continue weaving the bookmark if you have extra paper until there is very little left. Cut the ends into points.

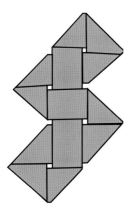

8 The completed model

Tip: Note how the little central squares alternate over and under all along the bookmark.

TRIANGULAR TRAYS

You can use two of these as inserts for a box or you can also use them as a small candy or nut dish.

You will need:

An 8 inches (20 cm) stiffened fabric square
Scissors

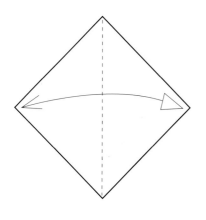

1 Begin with the paper side facing up. Valley fold in half diagonally from corner to corner. Then unfold.

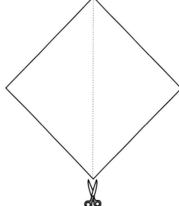

2 Cut along the crease you just made. You will have two triangles, each of which makes an insert.

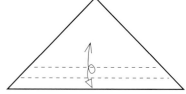

3 Take one of the triangles. Valley fold one edge down about half inch (1 cm). Then fold over again. Then unfold.

4 Repeat step 3 on the other two sides.

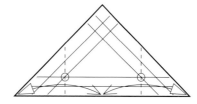

5 Note the circled points of intersection. Valley fold through those points perpendicular to the bottom edge. Then unfold.

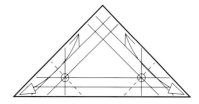

6 Note the circled points of intersection. Valley fold through those points perpendicular to the side edges. Then unfold.

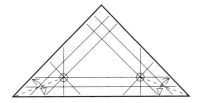

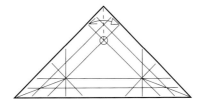

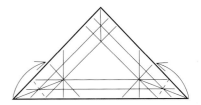

7 Note the circled points of intersection. Valley fold to those points, bisecting the angles. Then unfold.

8 Note the circled point of intersection. Valley fold to the points, bisecting the angle. Then unfold.

9 Valley fold the corners to the creases you made in step 6.

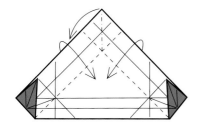

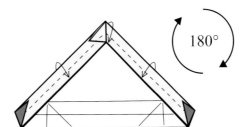

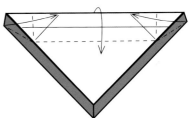

10 Bring the two sides up and bring the corner to the side. The model will not lie flat.

11 Wrap one layer down along the crease, locking it into place.

12 Bring the final side up and the two corners over, mountain folding from the intersection of the valley folds to the far corners.

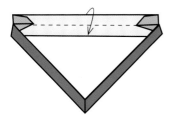

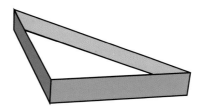

13 Valley fold the third side down, locking the two side corners.

14 The completed insert.

To make the other insert, fold the other triangle in the same way. The size given for the stiffened fabric will fit into a box that is 4 inches (10 cm) square.

BOTTLE WRAPPERS

Any bottle or round container can be dressed up with this simple cover. The suggested measurements are designed to fit over a wine bottle, but they can be adjusted to fit containers using the directions on the lower left of page 21.

You will need:

Bonded fabric 15 x 12 inches (38 x 30 cm) trimmed size
Scissors
Glue

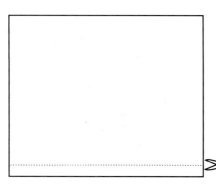

1 Cut one inch (2 cm) off one of the long edges for making the bow later on. Start with the paper side of the big piece of bonded fabric facing up.

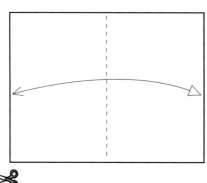

2 Valley fold the model in half. Then unfold.

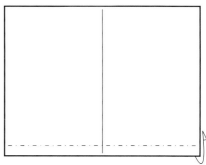

3 Mountain fold the long edge one inch (2 cm) to the back.

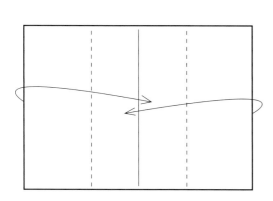

4 Valley fold both edges one inch (2 cm) beyond the center crease. They will overlap.

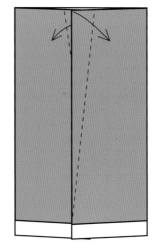

5 Valley fold the corners that are in the middle to the outside at an angle, to form the lapels.

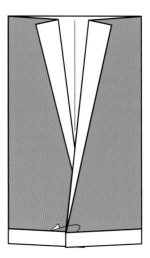

6 Slide the two sides of the bottom hem into each other. This forms a rounded, triangular column.

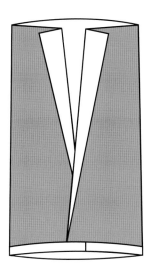

7 The completed main body.

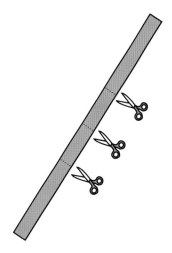

8 Valley 8. For the bow, cut the long strip (from step 1) into one piece five inches (12 cm) long and two pieces 2½ inches (6 cm) long. Discard the rest

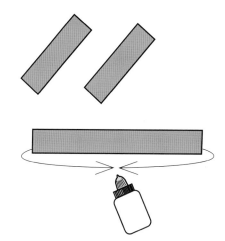

9 Double the longer piece and glue the ends together at the back.

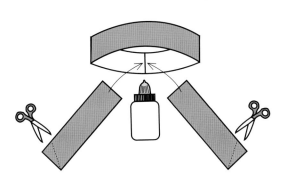

10 Glue the shorter pieces to the back. Cut the ends at a slant.

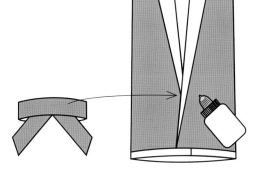

11 Glue the bow to the front of the main piece

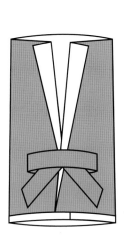

12 The completed bottle dress-up.

Other container sizes: To adjust the size of the cover to fit any round container, calculate the measurements like this:

For the short edges measure the height of the container.

For the long edges wrap a piece of paper around the container and add about 3 inches (8 cm).

These measurements result in the correct trimmed size of the bonded fabric. Don't forget to add extra room for the cutting.

GIFT BOX WITH PETAL TOP

The top of the finished box can be personalized by placing a photo, a Christmas ball, or keepsake between the four petals.

You will need:

For the lid: A square of fabric bonded to giftwrap, trimmed size 12 inches (30 cm) square

For the bottom: A square of fabric bonded to giftwrap, trimmed size 11½ inches (29 cm) square

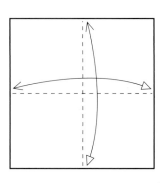

1 To make the lid, begin with the paper side facing up. Valley fold in half horizontally and vertically. Then unfold.

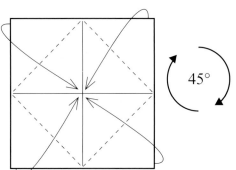

2 Valley fold the four corners to the center.

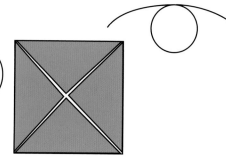

3 Flip the model over.

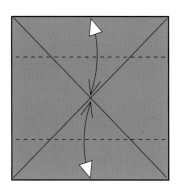

4 Fold the top and bottom edges to meet in the middle. Then unfold.

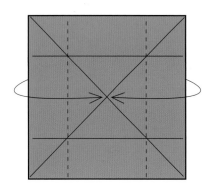

5 Fold the two side edges to meet in the middle.

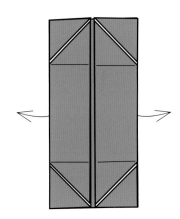

6 Release the corners from underneath to the sides.

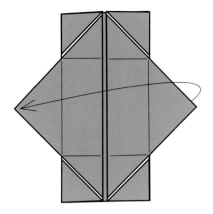

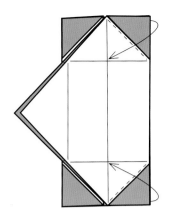

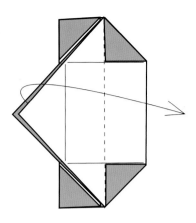

7 Swing the right triangular flap over to the left.

8 Fold the two corners to lie even with the center crease.

9 Valley fold the triangular flap back to its location in step 7.

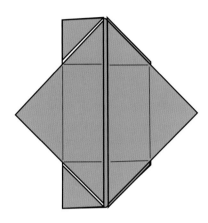

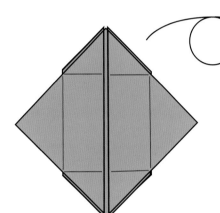

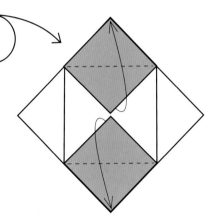

10 Repeat steps 7 – 9 on the left side.

11 Flip the model over.

12 Valley fold the central points to the corners.

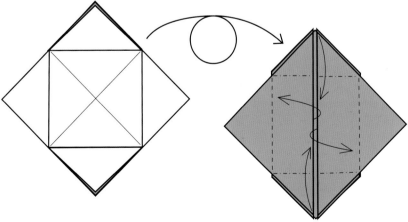

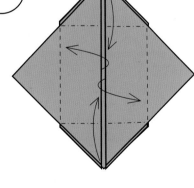

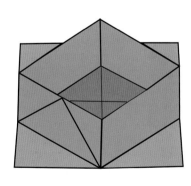

13 Flip the model over.

14 Spread the central layers, grasping both sides in the middle and pulling them to the right and left.

15 Turn the lid over.

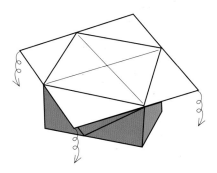 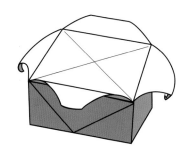 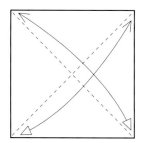

16 Curl the four corners (perhaps with a pencil).

17 The completed lid.

18 To make the bottom, begin with the paper side facing up. Valley fold in half both ways from corner to corner. Then unfold.

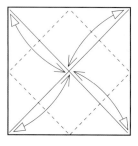 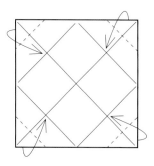 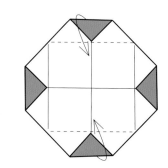

19 Valley fold the four corners to the center. Then unfold.

20 Valley fold the four corners to the nearest crease.

21 Valley fold two opposite corners along the creases you made in step 19.

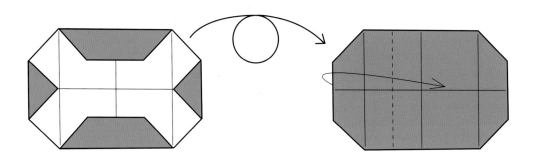

22 Flip the model over.

23 Valley fold one side over, creasing between the two vertical lines.

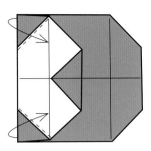

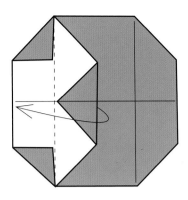

24 Valley fold the two corners to lie even with the center crease.

25 Valley fold the flap back to the edge.

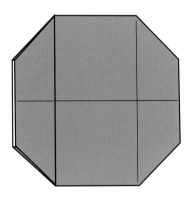

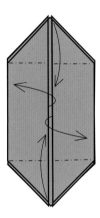

26 Repeat steps 23–25 on the other side.

27 Spread the central layers, grasping both sides in the middle and pulling them to the right and left.

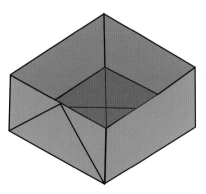

28 The completed bottom.

NOTEBOOKS

This little book is incredibly versatile; you can write a personal note or poem inside; or make it a small scrapbook, or glue some meaningful snapshots inside. Really, it's only limited by your imagination.

You will need:

A piece of stiffened fabric, 8½ inches x 11 inches(or A4)

A piece of printing paper, 8½ inches x 11 inches (or A4)—or a piece of paper 17 inches x 22 inches (60 cm x 21 cm)

Scissors

Tape

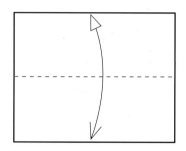

1 Begin with the piece of fabric. Fold the rectangle in half the long way. Then unfold.

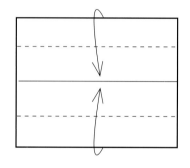

2 Valley fold the two sides nearly to the center.

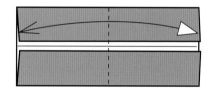

3 Valley fold in half. Then unfold.

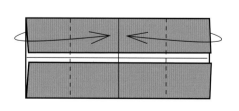

4 Valley fold the two sides nearly to the center.

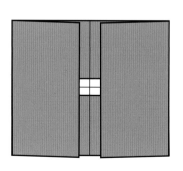

5 The completed cover unit.

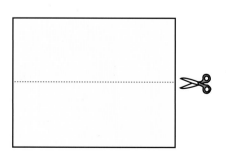

6 Cut the fabric in half the long way.

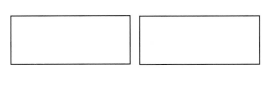

7 Tape the two short edges together.

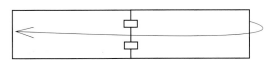

8 Fold the strip in half.

9 Repeat step 8 two more times. Then unfold back to the position you were in at the start of step 8.

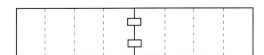

10 Pleat the strip, refolding it like a fan, alternating valley and mountain creases.

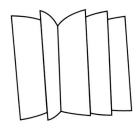

11 The completed pages unit.

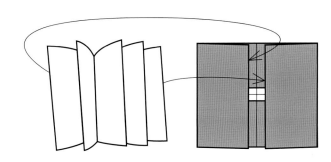

12 Insert the leftmost page into the left pocket and the rightmost page into the right pocket. The fabric may stick together but can be separated easily.

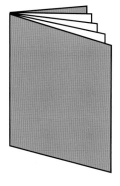

13 The completed book.

Tip: The given dimensions were chosen to take advantage of standard size paper for the pages, but these can be made in other sizes using the same proportions. For bigger books, it is best to fold separate sheets of paper in half and sew them together in the middle with large stitches.

EARRINGS

These earrings are simply fan-pleated from small squares. They can be made in just a few minutes from fabric scraps to coordinate with any outfit or to be wrapped up as a gift. Hardware for creating earrings can be found in most craft stores.

You will need:
A 3½ inches (9 cm) stiffened fabric squares
Earring fittings
Glue

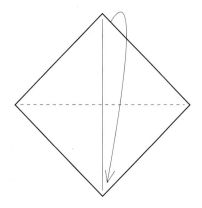

1 With the paper side facing up, fold the square on the diagonal into a triangle.

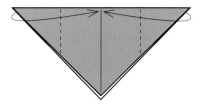

2 Valley fold both top corners to the middle of the top edge.

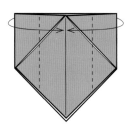

3 Valley fold the left and right edges to the center.

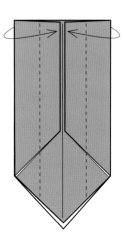

4 Valley fold the left and right edges to the center.

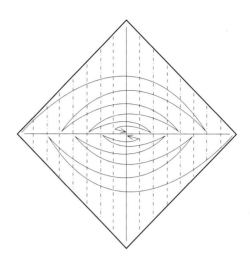

5 Completely unfold the model.

6 Fan pleat back and forth on the existing creases with alternating valley and mountain folds.

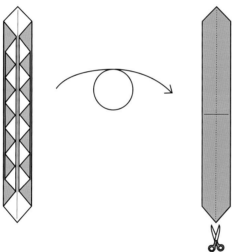

7 Flip the model over.

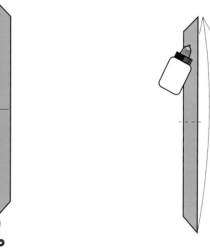

8 Cut the model in half along the longest crease. You will have two pleated triangles.

9 Fold vertically in half, gluing the top half to the bottom half, allowing the pleats to spread.

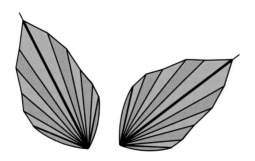

10 Attach earring fittings with glue.

PURSE

This purse, shaped like an envelope, has two compartments. The given dimensions will result in a purse size of 7½ x 6 inches (20 x 16 cm).

You will need:
A piece of sitffened fabric, 15 x 30 inches (40 x 80 cm)
Small piece of velcro to secure the triangular flap inside the front pocket
A cord at the sides of the purse for a strap

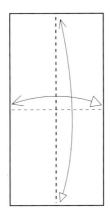

1 Begin with the inside of the fabric facing up. Valley fold in half horizontally and vertically. Then unfold.

2 Valley fold the four corners so that they lie even with the center crease.

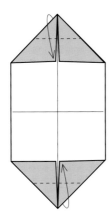

3 Valley fold the corners to the edge of the colored flaps.

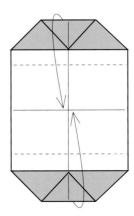

4 Valley fold both ends to meet in the center.

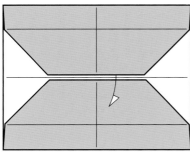

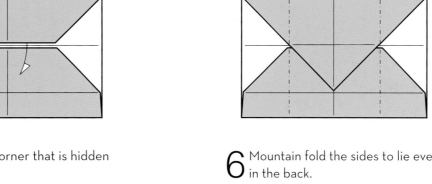

5 Pull out one corner that is hidden inside.

6 Mountain fold the sides to lie even in the back.

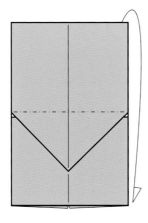

7 Mountain fold in half to the back.

8 The completed flat purse.

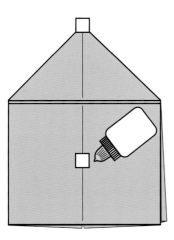

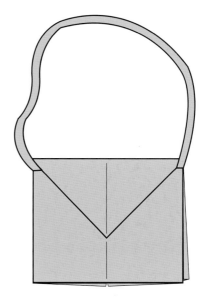

9 The triangular flap can be locked inside the front pocket or it can be secured with small pieces of velcro (as shown).

10 You can attach a cord at the sides of the purse for a strap.

FLOWERS WITH STEM

With the right kind of fabric these can make great party favors or you can make 12 of them and create an impressive bouquet of flowers.

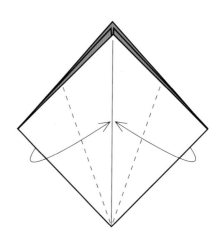

You will need:

Stiffened fabric, 5½ inches (14 cm) square
Glue
Scissors
A chenille stem (pipe cleaner)

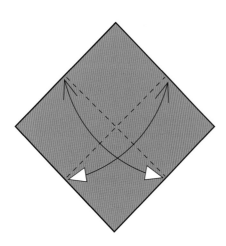

1 Begin paper side up. Valley fold the model from side to side in both directions.

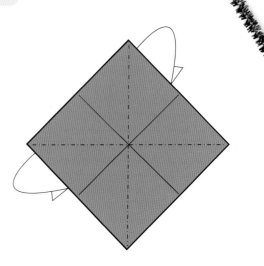

2 Mountain fold both sides behind from corner to corner. Then unfold.

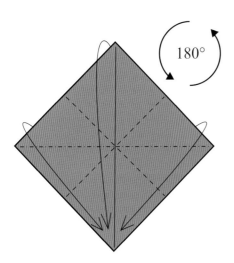

3 Squash the model into a preliminary base.

180°

Valley fold the two sides into the center. Repeat behind.

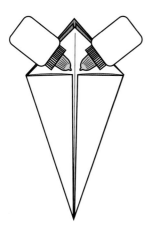
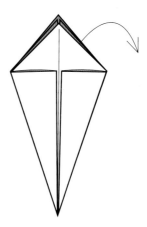

5 Put small drops of glue under the sides to hold the flower together. Repeat behind.

6 Poke your finger inside the flower and shape it into three dimensions. Roll the petals over a pen or pencil.

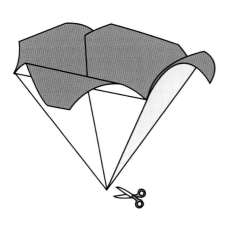

7 Snip off the tiniest bit from the bottom.

8 Curl one end of the chenille stem. Insert the other end into the flower from the top. The curled end will keep it in place.

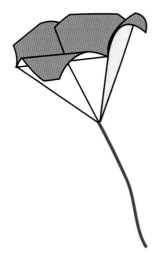

9 The completed flower.

GIFT POUCH

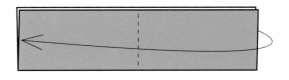

You will find many uses for this simple yet decorative envelope. You can use it as gift-wrap for flat items, such as scarves, ties, or a few greeting cards; or you can glue it into a scrapbook to hide a photo or personal message as a surprise.

Closure: You can lock the gift envelope with velcro.
For an extra touch, you can lock the envelope with one or two toothpicks.

> **You will need:**
> *A piece of fabric bonded to paper, 10 x 20 inches (25 x 50 cm)*
> *Scissors, Ruler, Pencil*
> *Optional: Velcro or toothpick*

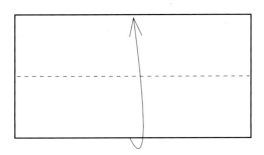

1 Start paper side up. Fold the piece in half the long way.

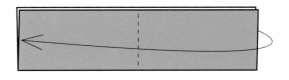

2 Fold the model in half the short way.

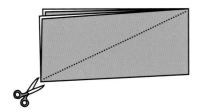

3 Cut the model from the bottom left corner to the top right corner.

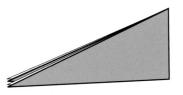

4 Completely unfold the model, once again with the paper side up.

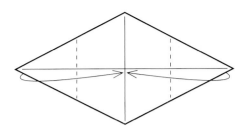

5 Valley fold the corners to the center.

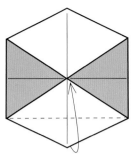

6 Valley fold the bottom corner to the center.

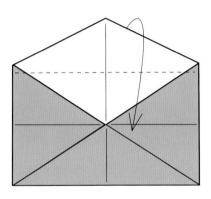

7 Valley fold the top down slightly past the center.

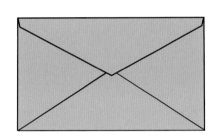

8 The completed gift envelope.

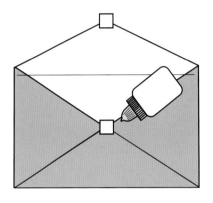

9 To lock the envelope, glue on small pieces of Velcro.

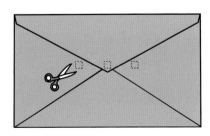

10 To lock the envelope using a toothpick, cut three small squares on the top layer as shown.

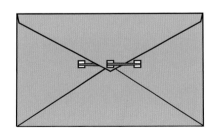

11 Then lock the envelope shut with a toothpick.

Tip: If you intend to make more than one gift envelope, consider making a paper template to cut out the diamond formed through steps 1–4.

GREETING CARDS

The tree on this greeting card is made with three units. They begin with a classic origami pattern, called the triangle (or waterbomb) base.

You will need:

Three fabric/paper squares with 2-, 2½-, 3-inch (5, 6.3, 7.6 cm) sides
Blank greeting card
Glue

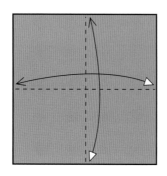

1 Begin with the outside of the fabric facing up. Valley fold in half horizontally and vertically. Then unfold.

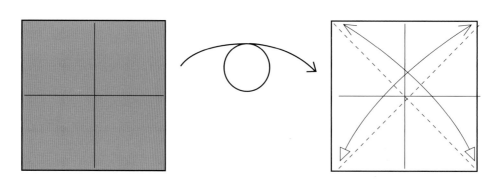

2 Turn the model over.

3 Valley fold the paper from corner to corner. Then unfold.

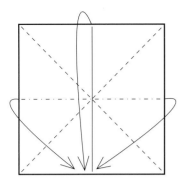 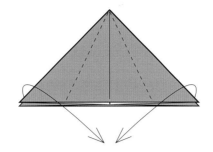 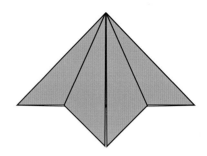

4 Collapse the model along its creases, forming a waterbomb base.

5 Valley fold the two sides of the front layer to lie even with the center crease.

6 The completed unit. Make the other two.

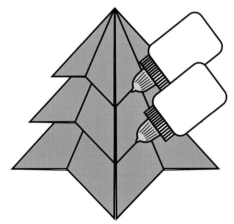 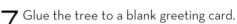 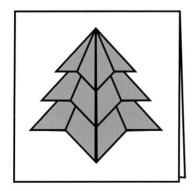

7 Glue the tree to a blank greeting card.

The completed greeting card.

HEXAGONAL BOX

Everybody loves boxes! The hexagonal box is one of our favorites and we have given many away as presents.

   The hexagon box is an example of origami unit folding, which means that similar units are combined for the end result. Two units form the lid and another two units form the bottom of the box. Most people find that the box is quite easy to make after having folded one or two. The given dimensions will result in a 5-inch (12 cm) box.

You will need:

For the bottom: 2 rectangles of bonded fabric, trimmed size 9 inches (22 cm) wide, 8 inches (20 cm) high

For the lid: 2 rectangles of bonded fabric, trimmed size 9½ inches (24 cm) wide, 7½ inches (19 cm) high

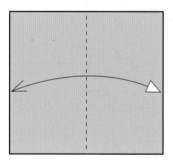

1 Begin fabric side up. Fold the rectangle in half, with the crease parallel to the shorter edges. Then unfold.

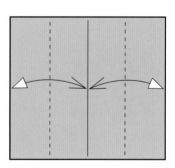

2 Fold the two sides into the center. Then unfold.

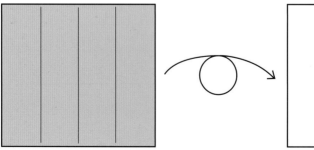

3 Flip the model over.

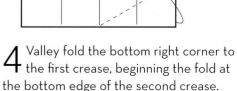

4 Valley fold the bottom right corner to the first crease, beginning the fold at the bottom edge of the second crease.

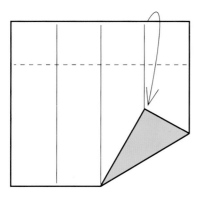

5 Valley fold the top edge down nearly to the corner.

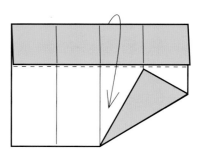

6 Valley fold the top edge down again.

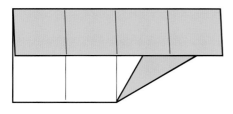

7 Undo the folds you made in steps 6 and 4, but not step 5.

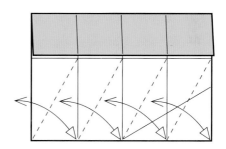

8 Valley fold the four rectangles on the diagonal, unfolding each time. The creases begin on the upper right corner of each rectangle and end on the bottom left corner.

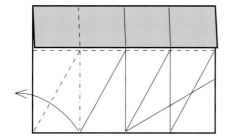

9 Grasp the leftmost vertical crease and swing it over along the valley you made in step 8. The model will not lie flat.

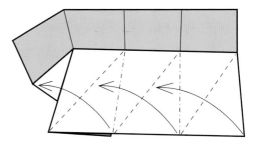

10 Repeat step 9 three more times.

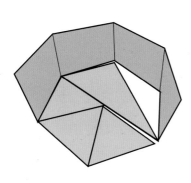

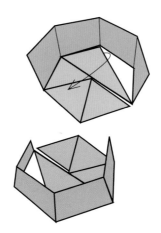

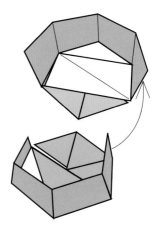

11 The completed unit. Fold three more using the assigned sizes.

12 Position two same-sized units as shown. Lift one flap on the top one.

13 Slide the rightmost flap on the bottom unit into the rightmost pocket of the top unit. Allow the base of the bottom unit to overlap those of the top unit.

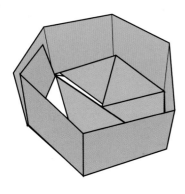

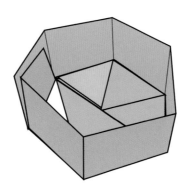

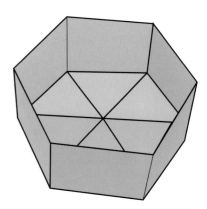

14 Reach into the model and pull up the flap that you folded down in step 12, returning it to its position in step 12. By doing so, you will tuck it over the bottommost layer of the bottom unit.

15 Repeat steps 13 and 14 on the other side. You may have to slide both units apart temporarily. This will be a little difficult to do, as it will involve rearranging layers.

16 Repeat the connection process on the other two same-sized units. The wider, shorter set is the lid and the narrower, taller set is the box.

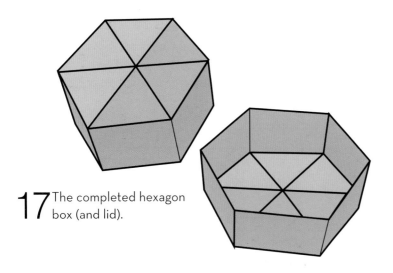

17 The completed hexagon box (and lid).

For calculating this box in other sizes, take the final size of the box in mind, then double it to obtain the width of the trimmed rectangle (this is approximate).

FOLDED NAPKINS

Fabric napkins folded into decorative shapes were featured in many cookbooks around the turn of the 19th century and were part of most dinner party table settings.

This elegant pattern that can be used as a table decoration, to wrap a special gift, or for holding a note. Also, its pocket can hold cutlery for a buffet table.

Napkins with the same color on both sides and not too light in weight are best—and there is no reason why you can't use paper napkins.

You will need:
A square napkin

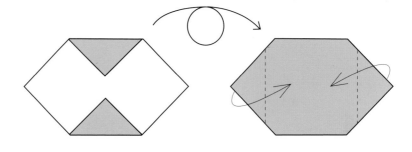

1 Start fabric side up. Valley fold two corners each about one inch (2 cm) from the center.

2 Flip the model over.

3 Valley fold the top and bottom corners each to one inch (2 cm) away from the center.

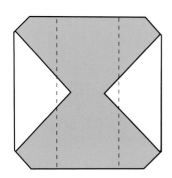
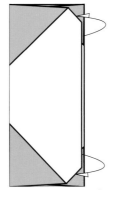
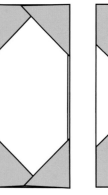

4 Valley fold the model into thirds, allowing the flaps to overlap.

5 Tuck the two right corners into the pockets behind them.

6 The completed folded napkin.

HOLIDAY CARDS

The holiday tree is made up of three units in graduated sizes. Each unit is folded from a square.

You will need:

Three stiffened fabric squares, 2½ inches square, 3 inches square, 3½ inches square (6, 8, and 10 cm squares)

5 inches or 7 inches (or A5) blank card

Glue

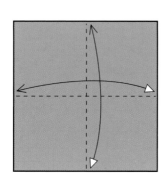

1 Begin with the outside of the fabric facing up. Valley fold in half horizontally and vertically. Then unfold.

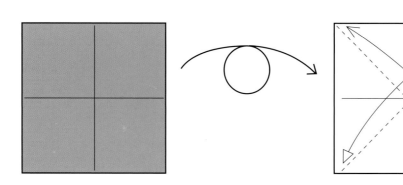

2 Turn the model over.

3 Valley fold the paper from corner to corner. Then unfold.

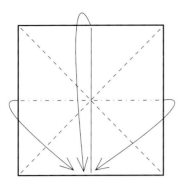 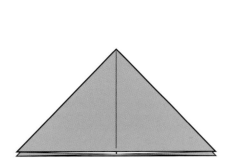 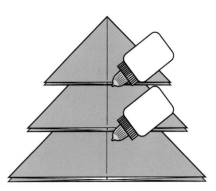

4 Collapse the model along its creases, forming a waterbomb base of the second crease.

5 The completed unit. Make the other two.

6 Glue the three units together, the largest on the bottom, the smallest on the top.

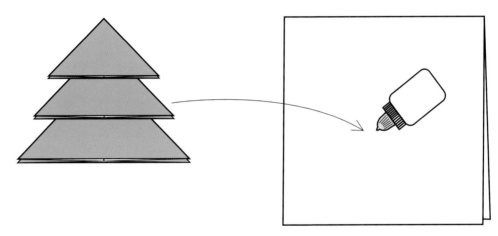

7 Glue the holiday tree to a blank greeting card.

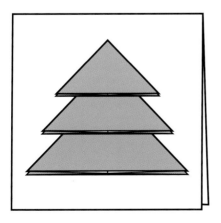

The completed holiday tree card!

KIMONO CARDS

Folding a kimono from stiffened fabric seems very appropriate, as it will reflect the texture of kimonos. It can be affixed to a blank greeting card. In our experience many origami cards are treasured by the recipients, who may even frame them. The dimensions in the instructions will result in a kimono 4 inches (10 cm) wide. You can make kimonos in other sizes by using bigger or smaller pieces of stiffened fabric in the proportion of three times as long as wide.

You will need:
A piece of stiffened fabric, 4 x 12 inches (10 x 30 cm)
Ruler
Glue
Blank Greeting card

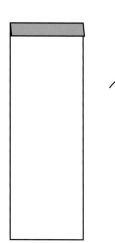

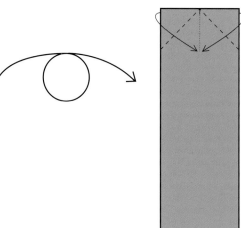

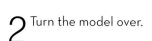

1 Begin with the inside of the fabric facing up. Valley fold the top edge over a small bit (about ⅜ inch/35 mm using the suggested size).

2 Turn the model over.

3 Pinch the top edge (or, if that will not show up, mark with a pencil or a small nick). Then valley fold both corners to the center, in line with the center pinch you just created.

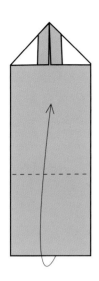

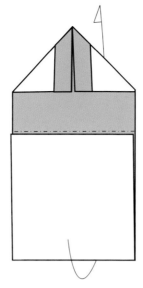

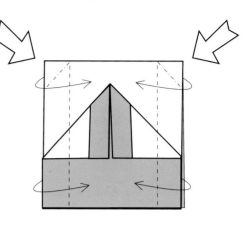

4 Valley fold four inches up from the bottom edge.

5 Mountain fold back along the edge you just folded up.

6 Bring both edges to lie even with the collar, squashing the top corners down.

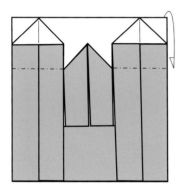

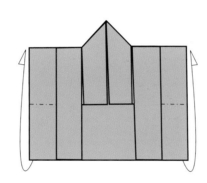

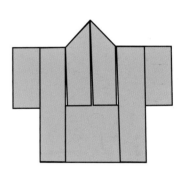

7 Mountain fold the top layer behind, leaving the pointed corner alone.

8 Mountain fold the bottom layer up to the top of the sleeves.

9 The completed kimono!

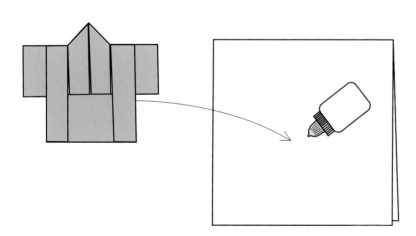

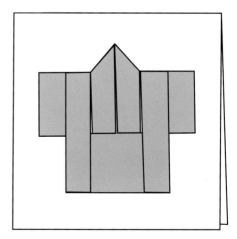

10 Glue the kimono to a blank greeting card.

The completed Kimono Card!

LOVE KNOTS

Love Knots are tokens of friendship that are long-lasting when made from fabric. They have a space inside for special notes for friends or it's a wonderful way to send affectionate greetings on Valentine's Day! Two people can use one love knot for sending messages back and forth by hiding a message written on a narrow strip of paper inside.

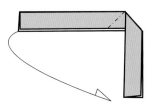

> **You will need:**
> A strip of stiffened fabric 20 x 4 inches (50 x 10 cm)
> Scissors

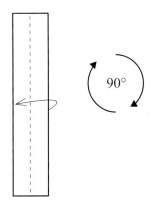

1 Begin with the inside of the fabric facing up. Fold the strip in half lengthwise.

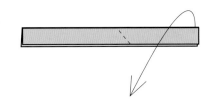

2 Valley fold one side down at a 90 degree angle.

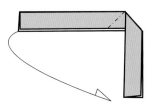

3 Mountain fold the other side behind at a 90 degree angle, meeting the other flap.

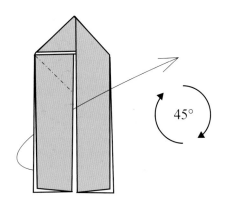

4 Mountain fold the flap behind at a 90 degree angle, pulling it in front of the first flap.

5 Cut the ends evenly into points.

6 The completed love knot.

POTTED PLANT GIFT WRAPPERS

This simple wrap will turn the gift of a plain potted plant into a more attractive presentation.

> ***You will need:***
> *A stiffened fabric square (suggested size for potted plants)*
> *A length of ribbon or raffia*

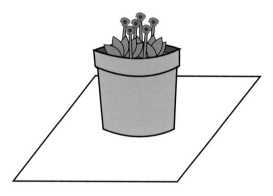

1 Place the potted plant in the center of the square.

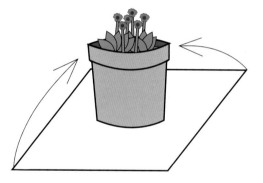

2 Lift up two opposite corners and hold them in place.

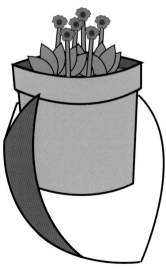

3 Lift up the other two corners and hold them in place.

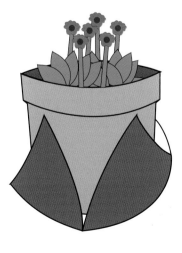

4 Wrap the length of ribbon or raffia around the pot, locking the cover in place.

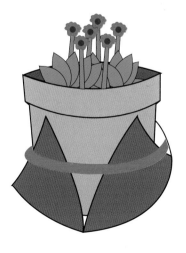

5 The completed plant pot cover.

NAPKIN RINGS

This ring can be adjusted to fit the bulk of different napkins.

You will need:
A 6 inches (15 cm) square of stiffened fabric

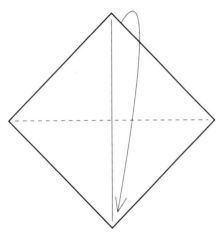

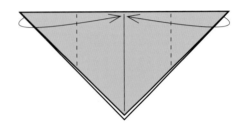

1 With the paper side facing up, fold the square on the diagonal into a triangle.

2 Valley fold both top corners to the middle of the top edge.

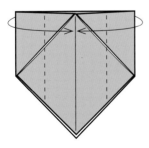

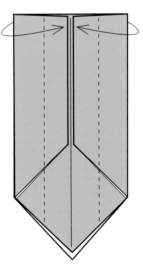

3 Valley fold the left and right edges to the center.

4 Valley fold the left and right edges to the center.

5 Completely unfold the model.

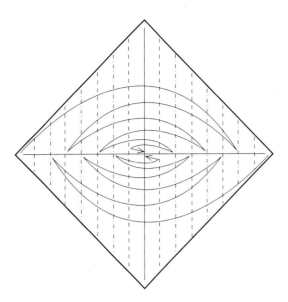

6 Fan pleat back and forth on the existing creases with alternating valley and mountain folds.

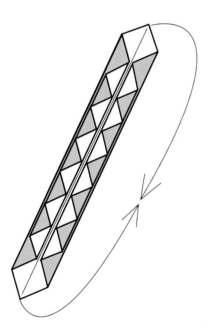

7 Wrap the strip in a loop, tucking one end into the other so that the pattern continues evenly. For a smooth fit you may have to narrow one end a little bit.

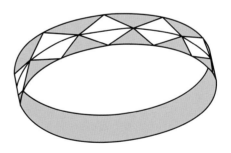

8 The completed napkin ring.

LITTLE BIRDS

This Little Bird is a very popular, traditional origami figure in Spain, where it is called "pajarita" (Little Bird). It is reproduced in many guises, such as oversized sculptures and in advertisements.

This can be a charming gift for displaying on a shelf or a desk. It involves quite a few folding steps, but none are difficult.

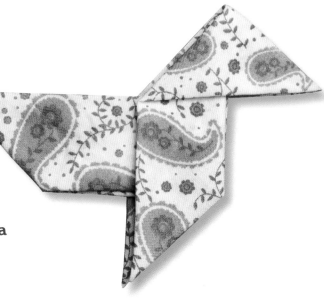

You will need:
A stiffened fabric square—An 8 inches (20 cm) square produces a 5-inch (13 cm) long bird

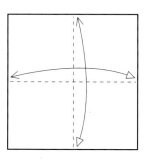

1 Begin with the outside of the fabric facing up. Valley fold in half horizontally and vertically. Then unfold.

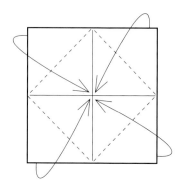

2 Valley fold all four corners to the center.

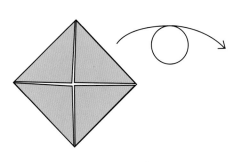

3 Flip the model over.

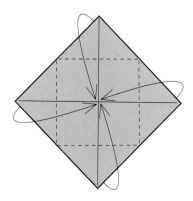

4 Valley fold all four corners to the center.

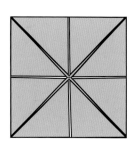

5 Flip the model over.

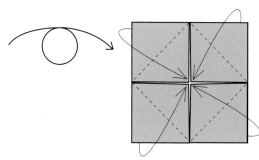

6 Valley fold all four corners to the center.

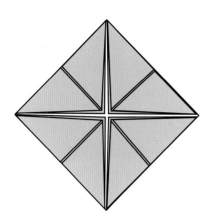

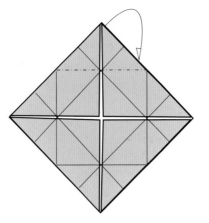

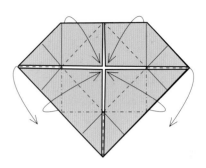

7 Unfold to your position in step

8 Mountain fold the top corner behind.

9 Collapse according to the given creases, bringing the edges into the center. See next step for details.

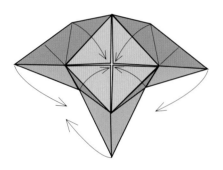

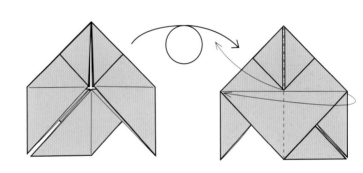

10 Continue collapsing.

11 Flip the model over.

12 Valley fold the model in half, while swinging top point up and out.

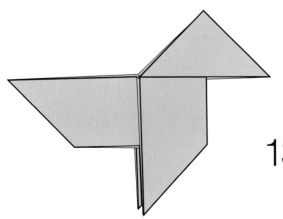

13 The completed Little Bird (pajarita).

PEACOCK

This cloth sculpture is a great way to display a beautiful fabric pattern using a bird fold that is less common than the typical crane or penguin folds.

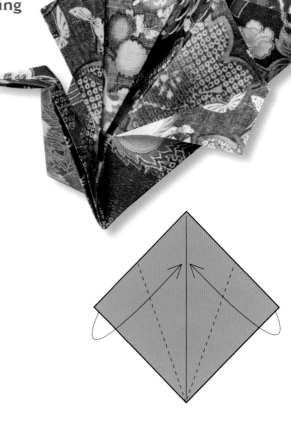

> ### You will need:
>
> A bonded fabric square
> Rough size: 11 inches (27 cm)
> Trimmed size: 10 inches (25 cm)

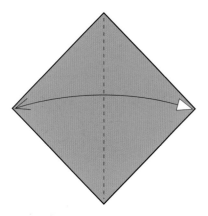

1 Begin with the fabric side facing up. Valley fold in half from corner to corner. Then unfold.

2 Valley fold two adjacent sides to lie even with the center crease. This is called a kite fold.

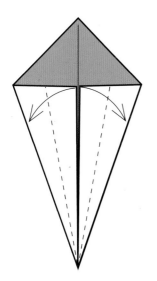

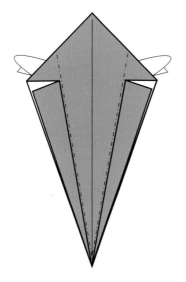

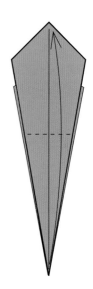

3 Valley fold the two center edges to lie even with the sides.

4 Mountain fold to the back along the creases made in step 3.

5 Valley fold the bottom corner to the top corner.

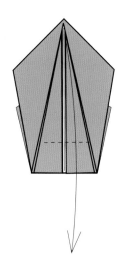

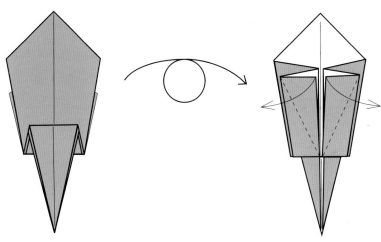

6 Valley fold the flap back down (though not all the way).

7 Flip the model over.

8 Valley fold the two corners out as far as they will go.

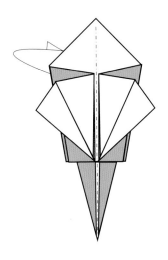

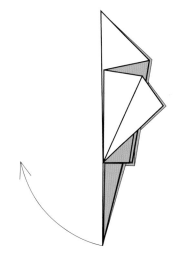

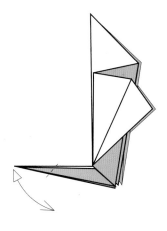

9 Mountain fold the model in half.

10 Pull the neck out at an angle, making a sharp crease at the bottom.

11 Valley fold the neck flap, creasing what will become the head. Then unfold.

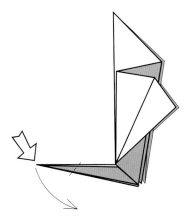

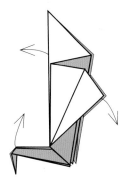

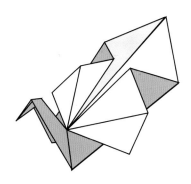

12 Inside reverse fold the neck along the crease you made in step 11. This forms the head.

13 Spread the layers, pulling the head up and separating the tail. The model will not lie flat.

14 The completed peacock.

PICTURE FRAMES

The size given for this frame will fit an 8 x 10 inches (20 x 25 cm) photograph. To make the frame for other sizes, just use a piece of fabric one inch (2.5 cm) larger on each size than the photo.

You will need:
One square of paper bonded to fabric, suggested size 10 x 12 inches (26 x 30 cm)

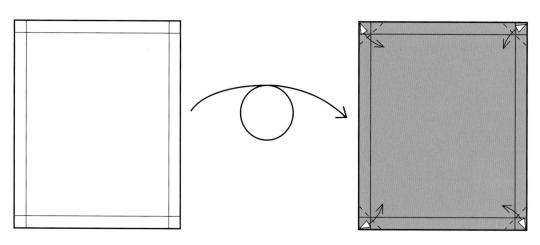

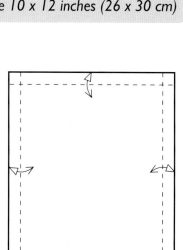

1 Start paper side up. Valley fold each side in about an inch. Then unfold.

2 Flip the model over.

3 Valley fold the four corners in, so that the creases intersects with the lines you made in step 1.

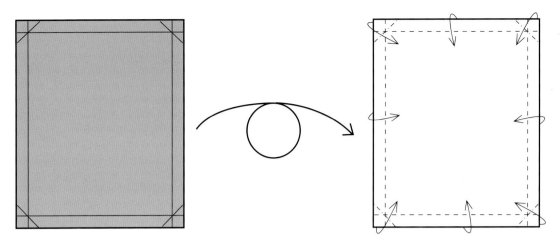

4 Flip the model over.

5 Collapse the four sides in along the precreases.

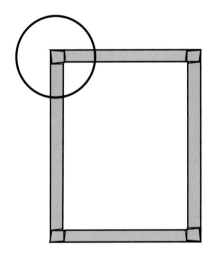

6 The next couple step zooms in on one corner.

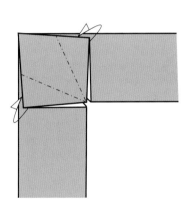

7 Mountain fold two edges behind, locking the corner. The next step will be zoomed out again.

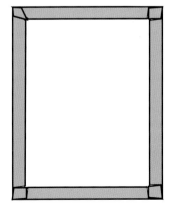

8 Repeat step 7 on the other three corners.

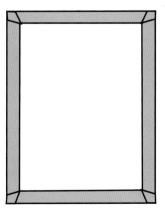

9 The completed picture frame.

FRAMED ROSE

In nature, each layer of a rose is made up of five petals. We have taken this fact as inspiration for this flower picture. The rose is folded from a piece of bonded fabric in the shape of a pentagon that you can cut easily with the help of the template. The size shown will result in a 4-inch (10 cm) rose. For a larger rose, enlarge the template and follow the instructions in the same way.

You will need:

Rose-colored bonded fabric, 8 inches (20 cm) from corner to corner in a pentagon shape or cut one from 8 x 10 inches (20 x 25 cm) fabric square

Cardboard (cut slightly larger than the original paper square, i.e. 8¾ inches/22 cm)

Royal blue velvet (slightly larger than the cardboard)

Scissors

Glue

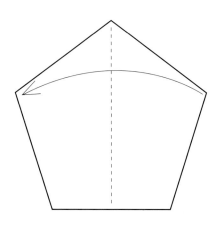

1 Begin with the paper side facing up. Fold the pentagon in half.

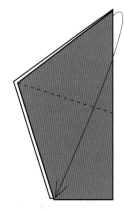

2 Valley fold the top corner to lie even with the bottom corner.

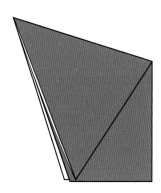

3 Unfold the pentagon. The two creases intersect at the center.

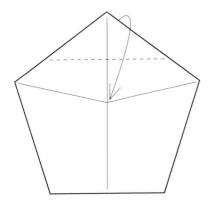

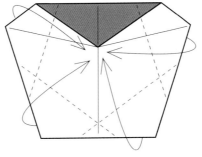

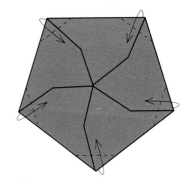

4 Fold a corner to the center intersection.

5 Fold the other four corners to the center. They will overlap.

6 Valley fold the corners in about ¾ inch (2 cm). Do not fold them in all the way; rather, let them stand up.

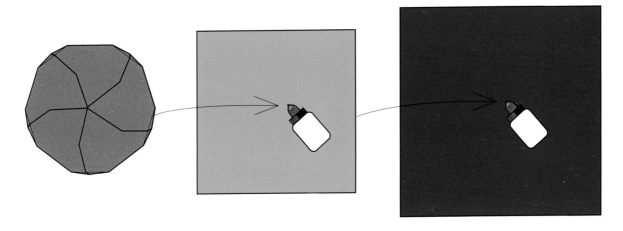

7 The completed rose.

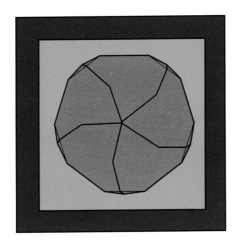

8 The completed rose picture.

EASTER BUNNY

This fabric bunny can be a lively addition to any Easter basket. Use a pastel fabric that celebrates the season.

You will need:

A square of stiffened fabric—A 6-inch (15 cm) square results in a 3-inch (7 cm) bunny

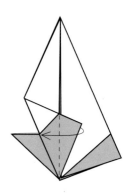

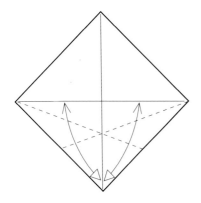

1 Start color side up. Fold the two bottom edges up to the center crease. Then unfold.

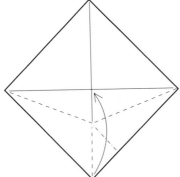
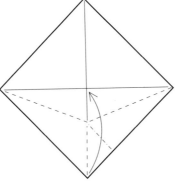

2 Squash the bottom corner in to the center, forming half of a simple fish base.

3 Flip the model over.

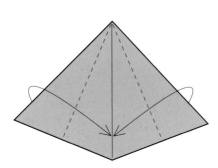

4 Valley fold the left and right sides of the model into the center crease.

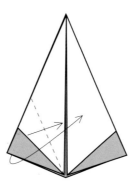

5 Valley fold the bottom left edge of the model up and to the center, aligning where the white meets the colored part of the paper with the center crease.

6 Valley fold the flap back over across the center crease.

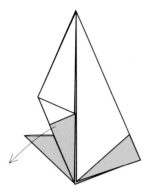

7 Unfold back to step 5.

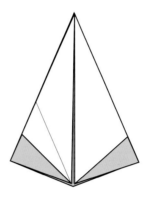

8 Repeat steps 5–7 on the other side.

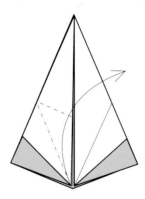

9 Swing the left flap up and across.

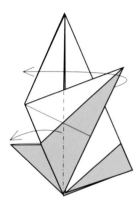

10 Squash the flap across along its central crease.

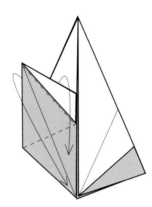

11 Squash the flap down, using the creases you made in steps 5–8.

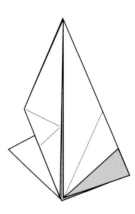

12 Repeat steps 9–11 on the other side.

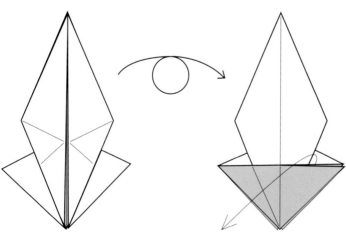

13 Flip the model over.

14 Pull forward the triangular white flap, opening up the bottom of the model.

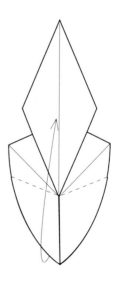

15 Collapse the flap back so that it lies flat.

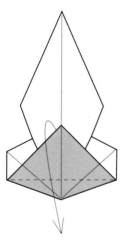

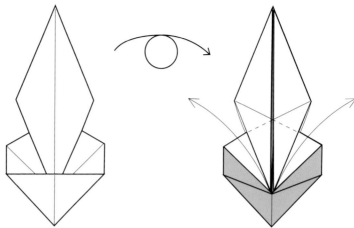

16 Valley fold the flap down as far as it will go.

17 Flip the model over.

18 Valley fold the two colored flaps up and out as far as they will go.

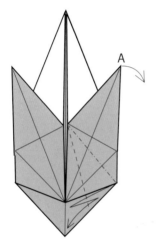

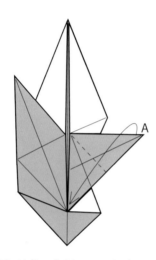

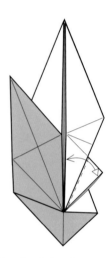

19 Swivel point A to the right and down, making a mountain and valley fold.

20 Valley fold point A down as far as it will go.

21 Valley fold the flap up along the edge. Then unfold.

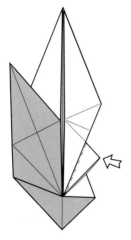

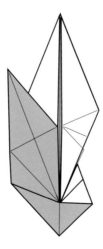

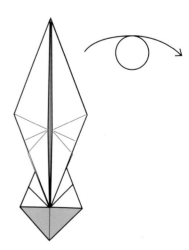

22 Reverse fold the flap inside along the crease you made in step 21.

23 Repeat steps 19–22 on the other side.

24 Flip the model over.

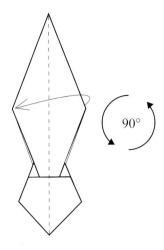

25 Valley fold the model in half.

26 Valley fold the flap as far over as it will go. Repeat behind.

27 Inside reverse fold the end of the model. Repeat behind.

28 Squash the flap up, spreading the layers apart (see next step for details). Repeat behind.

29 Collapse the flap back down. Repeat behind.

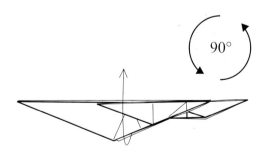

30 Open the model up, bringing it to the same position it was in, back in step 25.

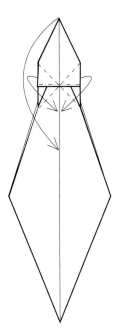  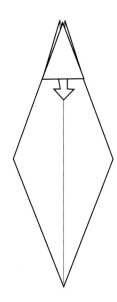

31 Collapse the bottom of the model up, bringing the two sides in to the center.

32 Valley fold the top of the flap you just created down to the bottom.

33 Unsink the center of the small group of layers.

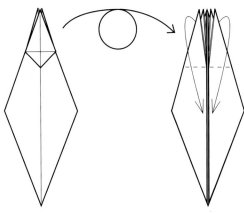

34 Flip the model over.

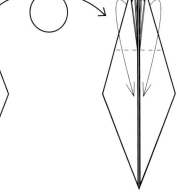

35 Valley fold the top two flaps down.

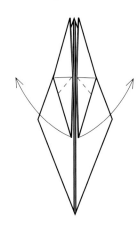

36 Valley fold the two points up at their angle bisectors.

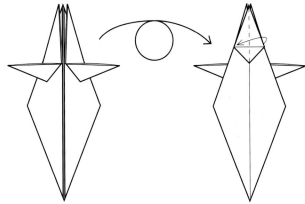 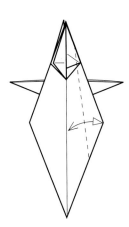

37 Valley fold the two points up at their angle bisectors.

38 Valley fold one layer over to the left.

39 Valley fold right side into the center. Then unfold.

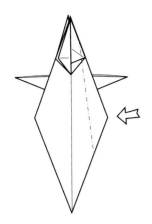

40 Closed sink along the crease you made in step 39.

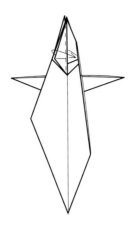

41 Valley fold one layer back to the right.

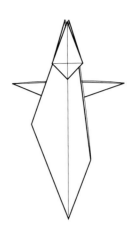

42 Repeat steps 38–41 on the left.

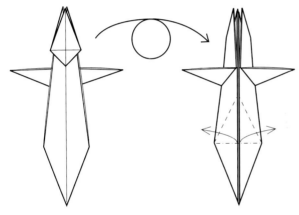

43 Flip the model over.

44 Spread the layers in the center, squashing them out.

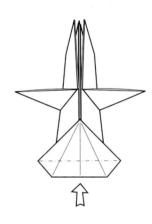

45 Closed sink the bottom layer up.

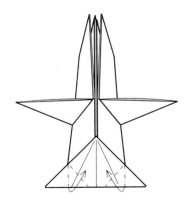

46 Squash both corners up.

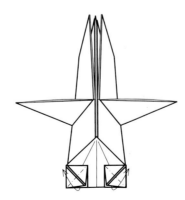

47 Spread the center layers apart, bringing the points up.

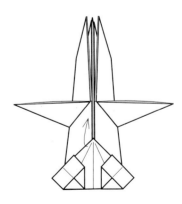

48 Pull up the corner, spreading the layers. The model will not lie flat.

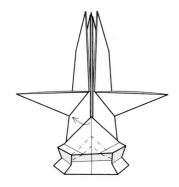

49 Squash the corner up as shown.

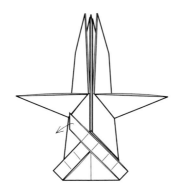

50 Pull down the corner that will become the tail, performing slight valley folds.

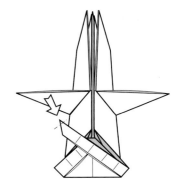

51 Sink the tip of the tail.

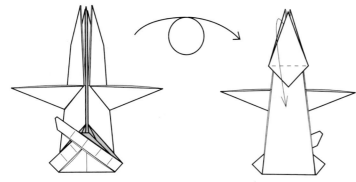

52 Flip the model over.

53 Valley fold the top corner down as far as it will go.

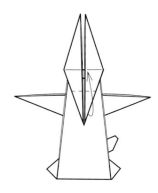

54 Valley fold the corner up to the center crease.

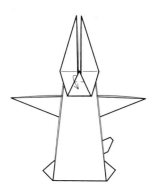

55 Valley fold the tip down.

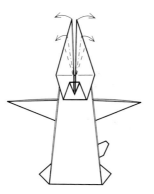

56 Squash the ears apart slightly.

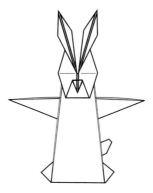

57 Shape the model, spreading the ears slightly, rounding the nose and arms.

58 The completed model.

MAGIC WANDS

We all need a little magic in our lives and this Magic Wand makes a wonderful decoration item that can match a color scheme or a party theme.

You will need:
Stiffened fabric, 8 x 20 inches
  (20 cm x 50 cm)
Wire twist or rubber band or thread
Glue
Dowel or chopstick
Sticky tape

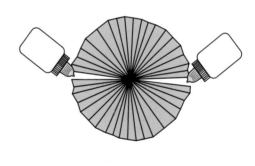

1 Valley fold the shorter side over a little bit.

2 Mountain fold the flap behind.

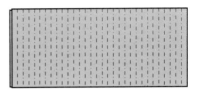

3 Repeat this pleating process across the rest of the model.

4 Tie the pleat together at the center with the wire twist. Allow the ends to hang freely.

5 Spread the fabric paper into a pleated circle.

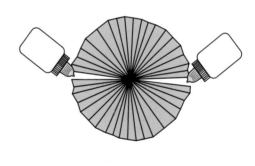

6 Glue both ends together.

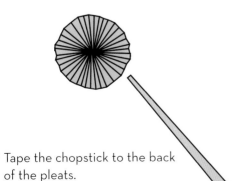

7 Tape the chopstick to the back of the pleats.

8 The completed magic wand.

Decorations: Glue on glitter or sequins. Tie on lengths of ribbon.

THANKSGIVING TURKEY DECORATIONS

This unique fold will give the Thanksgiving cornucopia some additional pizzazz. Use fall colors to match the pumpkins and corn; or use these as place setting favors.

You will need:
A square of stiffened fabric
A 6 inches (15 cm) square results in
   a 4 inches (9 cm) turkey

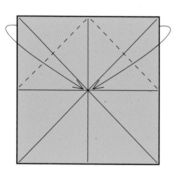

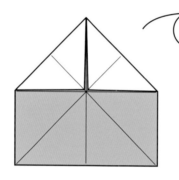

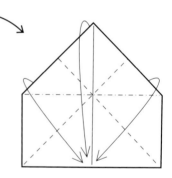

1 Start color side up. Valley fold two adjacent corners into the center.

2 Flip the model over.

3 Squash the model into half of a preliminary base.

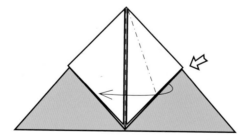

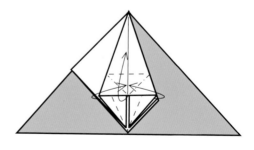

4 Squash one flap over, so that what was formerly the edge of the flap lies even with the center crease.

5 Petal fold the flap up.

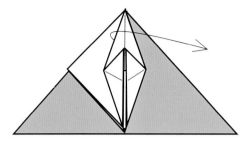

6 Unwrap some paper the around center flap, collapsing according to pre-creases.

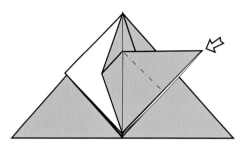

7 Squash the flap down into half of a preliminary base.

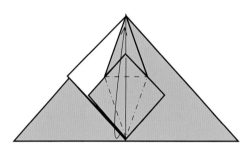

8 Petal fold the bottom up, forming half a bird base.

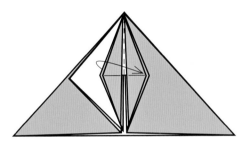

9 Valley fold the right flaps over.

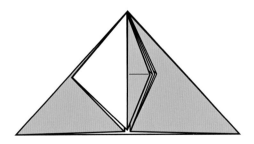

10 Repeat steps 4–8 on the left side.

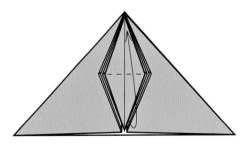

11 Valley fold the bottom point up as far as it will go.

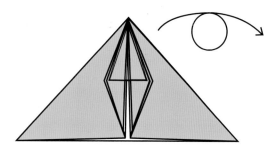

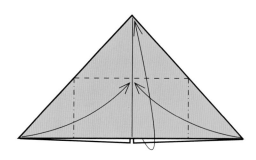

12 Flip the model over.

13 Squash the bottom edge up to lie even with the top, bringing the sides into the center.

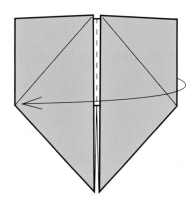

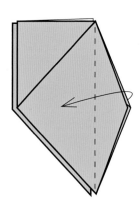

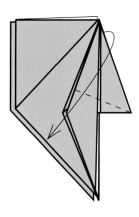

14 Valley fold one layer over.

15 Valley fold two more layers over.

16 Valley fold the top point down along its edge.

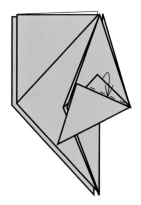

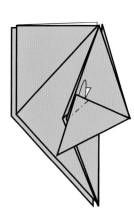

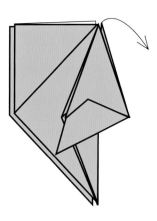

17 Valley fold the flap behind as shown.

18 Mountain fold the edge of the wing behind into the pocket.

19 Pull the flap out slightly, collapsing it down.

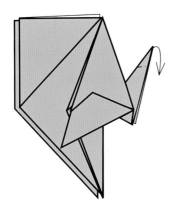

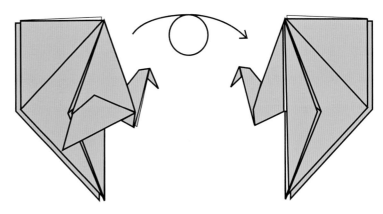

20 Reverse fold the tip down, creating the head.

21 Flip the model over.

22 Repeat steps 15–17 on this side.

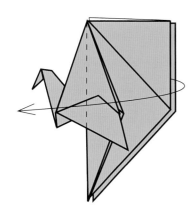

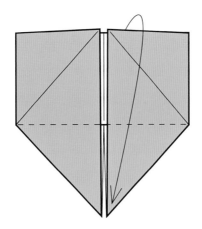

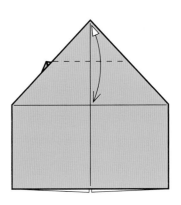

23 Valley fold two layers over to the right.

24 Valley fold the top layer down all the way.

25 Valley fold the top point in to the center. Then unfold.

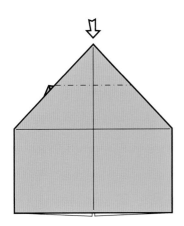

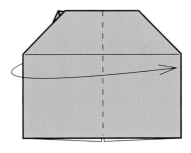

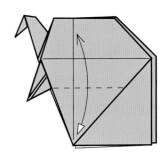

26 Open sink the top point along the crease made in step 24.

27 Valley fold one layer over to the right.

28 Valley fold the bottom point up, creasing where the wing meets the body. Then unfold.

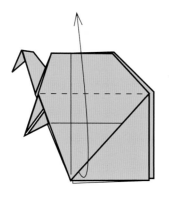

29 Valley fold the bottom point up as far as it will go.

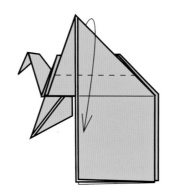

30 Valley fold the top point down along the crease you made in step 27.

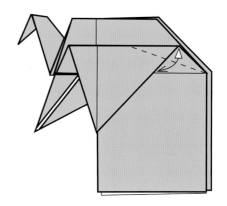

31 Valley fold right side of the flap down to the crease. Then unfold.

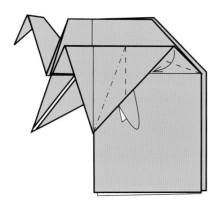

32 Bring the right side into the center, squashing along the crease you made in step 30.

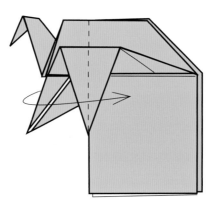

33 Valley fold one layer over to the right.

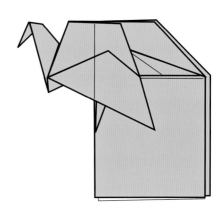

34 Repeat steps 27–32 behind.

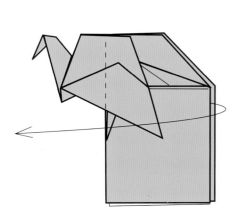

35 Valley fold two layers over to the left.

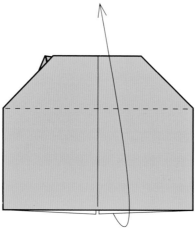

36 Valley fold one layer over to the right.

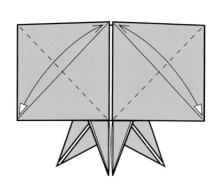

37 Valley fold bottom corners to the top center. Then unfold.

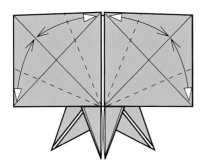

38 Valley fold through all layers, bringing the edges to lie even with the crease you made in step 36. Then unfold.

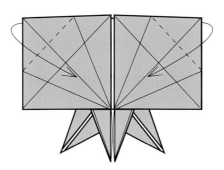

39 Valley fold the top corners in using the creases you made in step 37 as landmarks.

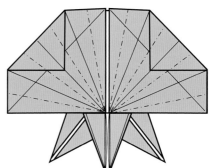

40 Mountain fold through all layers, between the valley creases you made. Then unfold.

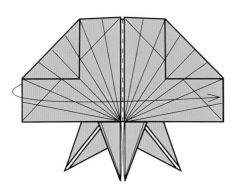

41 Valley fold two layers back to the right.

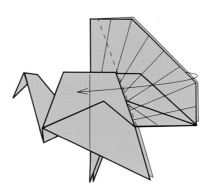

42 Valley fold the back flap forward along the edge of the wing. Don't fold the wing forward all the way. Rather, the model will not lie flat. Repeat behind.

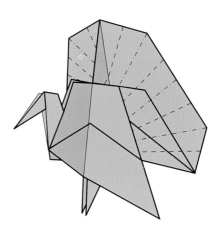

43 Pleat the tail slightly along the pre-creases, fanning it.

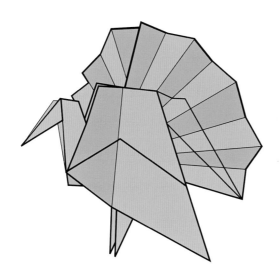

44 The completed model.

STANDING CATS

The cat stands up if you unfold the tail. Open the whole body, and wrap the tail around the front and back while closing the body. This procedure is called an "outside reverse fold."

Cat lovers everywhere will enjoy receiving gifts, letters, invitations, and holiday cards decorated with these origami cats. You might want to experiment using different types of colored and patterned paper, and drawing in the eyes, nose, and whiskers with a felt tip pen.

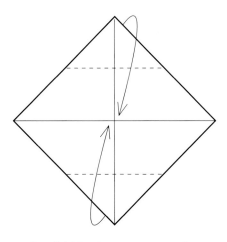

You will need:
One 8 inches (20 cm) stiffened fabric square
One 6 inches (15 cm) stiffened fabric square

Head

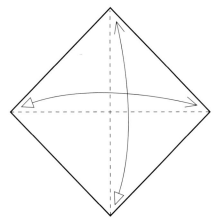

1 Begin with the outside of the fabric facing up. Valley fold in half diagonally both ways. Then unfold.

2 Valley fold both corners into the center.

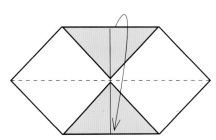

3 Valley fold the model in half.

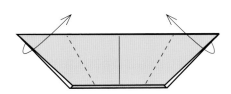

4 Valley fold the sides up to form the ears.

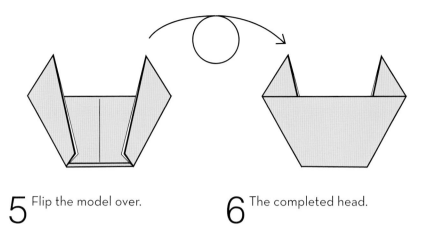

5 Flip the model over.

6 The completed head.

Body 7

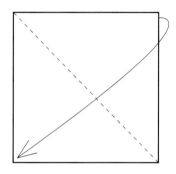

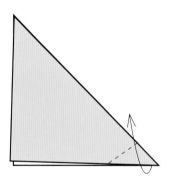

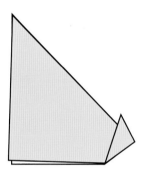

7 Begin with the outside of the fabric facing up. Valley fold in half diagonally.

8 Valley fold the bottom right corner up slightly to form the tail.

9 The completed body.

Assembly 10

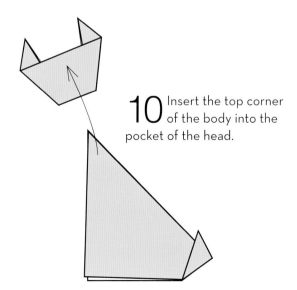

10 Insert the top corner of the body into the pocket of the head.

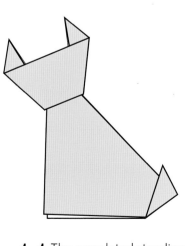

11 The completed standing cat.

SANTA CLAUS

This cloth Santa Claus has many kinds of
uses during the holiday gift giving season.
You can place it on a package, use it as an
ornament, or make it a stocking stuffer.

You will need:

*A square of stiffened fabric—A 6-inches (15 cm) square
results in a 4-inches (9 cm) St. Nick*

1 Start white side up. Valley fold
the four corners of the model
into the center, forming a blintz
base.

2 Flip the model over.

3 Fold each of the sides into the
center line.

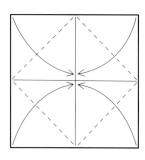
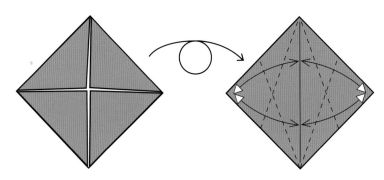
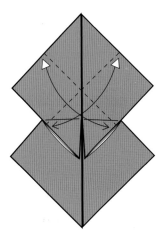
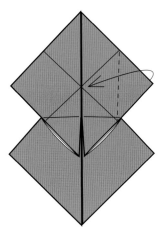
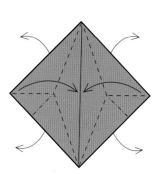

4 Squash each of the opposite
corners in to the center, forming a simple fish base, but swinging
the four flaps out from underneath.

5 Perform two valley folds, creasing only the top layer.

6 Valley fold the right corner into
the center.

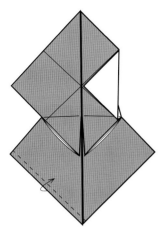

7 Valley fold the left side up slightly.

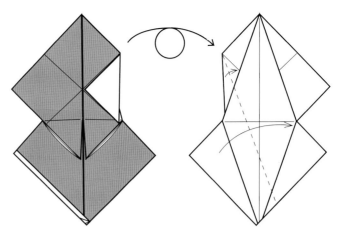

8 Flip the model over.

9 Valley fold the left edge to the crease you made in step 5 at the angle bisector. Then unfold.

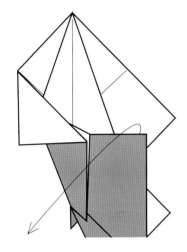

10 Undo the fold you made in step 9.

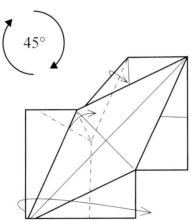

45°

11 Valley fold the left edge to the crease you made in step 5 at the angle bisector. Then unfold.

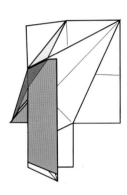

12 Step 11 shown in progress.

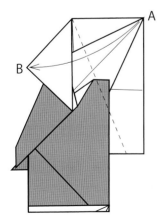

A

B

13 Valley fold point A to point B.

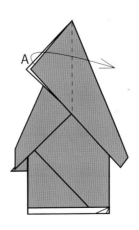

A

14 Valley fold point A back across.

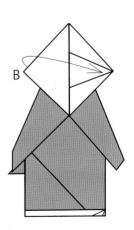

B

15 Valley fold point B across.

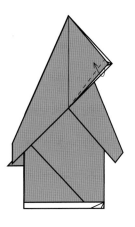

16 Valley fold the point up slightly.

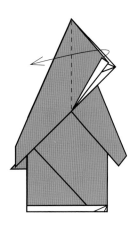

17 Valley fold the point back.

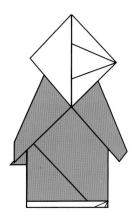

18 Repeat steps 15–17 on the right side.

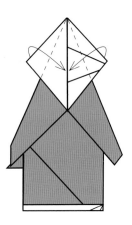

19 Valley fold the top edges into the center.

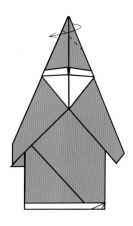

20 Valley fold the tip of the hat down slightly.

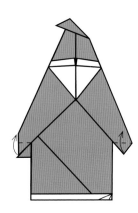

21 Valley fold the paper up on the right arm; wrap it up and around on the left arm.

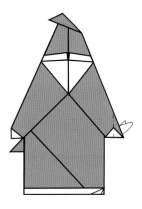

22 Mountain fold the tip of the right hand behind.

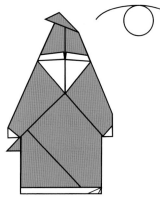

23 Mountain fold the tip of the right hand behind, making it look like the left.

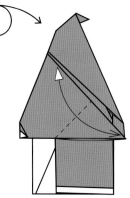

24 Valley fold the point up as far as it will go. Then unfold.

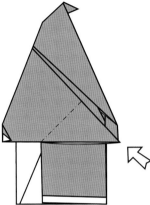

25 Inside reverse fold the point along the crease you made in step 20.

26 Shape the top of the model, pulling sides down as shown.

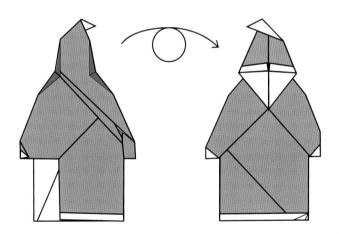

27 Flip the model over. 28 The completed model.

POCKET ROCKET

This is a very simple fold for a beginner. The rectangular size of the cloth makes it easy to use scraps that won't work on projects that require squares.

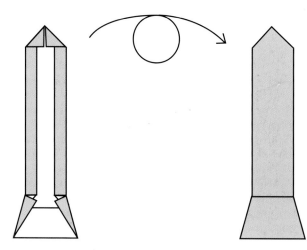

You will need:
A 3 x 11 inches (8 x 28 cm) strip of stiffened fabric

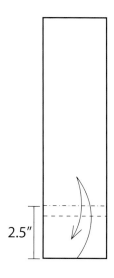

2.5"

1 Begin with the outside of the fabric facing up. Make a pleat by folding mountain and valley folds (i.e. fold flap down, then back up).

2 Valley fold the two small corners.

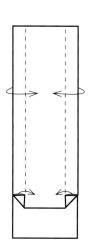

3 Open two small corners and squash flat while folding side edges in. Two triangles should form at the base of the rocket. Don't fold the lower part of the paper.

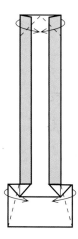

4 Fold corners in at the top and bottom as shown.

5 Flip the model over.

6 The completed space rocket.

JAN 31 2014